# Cybernetic

## Cybersecurity Types, Threats, and Tips

## Epris E Ezekiel

# Contents

Origin ............................................................. 1

Chapter 1 ...................................................... 5

What is Cybersecurity? ................................... 5

Chapter 2 .................................................... 10

Cyberthreat categories ................................. 10

Chapter 3 .................................................... 19

How to Install a Secure Network at Home ................... 19

Chapter 4 .................................................... 37

Effects of Cyberattacks on Businesses ............ 37

Chapter 5 .................................................... 42

Why Cybersecurity Matters ........................... 42

Chapter 6 .................................................... 47

The Protective Role of Cybersecurity Experts ............. 47

Chapter 7 .................................................... 50

Future Prospects for Cybersecurity ............... 50

# Origin

Most internet users have now been impacted by cybercrime in one way or another. Whether it was a malware attack on your home or work computer, a website you frequent, or a breach in cybersecurity, you have probably encountered some cybercrime.

It can be startling to consider how recent the developments of cybersecurity and computer hacking are, even if they seem like they are discussed often these days. You don't have to travel very far to reach the early days of cereal whistles and college students. The pace at which the advances have advanced has been steadily growing since then.

The first known cyberattack happened in France in 1834, according to technical standards. Through French Telegraph System hacking, two thieves took financial market information. Not until 1940 did things start to get intriguing, but other "hackers" would later arise to cause disruptions in wireless telegraphy and phone services.

Rene Carmille emerged as the pioneer of ethical hacking in 1940. In France during the Nazi occupation, he was an expert on punch-card computers and a member of the Resistance. He was the owner of the information processing devices utilized by the Vichy government in France. He realized that the Nazis were utilizing the devices to track out Jews, so he offered to allow them to use his equipment. After they fell for the bait, he exploited their access to hack them and thwart their plans.

It's fascinating to learn about cybersecurity history. The virus is said to have been generated and spread in 1971 by Bob Thomas, a BBN computer programmer, as a security test. While not malevolent, it did draw attention to weak points and security vulnerabilities in the development of what would eventually become "the internet."

The virus was created to spread over ARPANET (Advanced Research Projects Agency Network), the precursor to what is now known as the internet. It was named after the evil character "Creeper" from Scooby Doo. The U.S. Department of Defense established ARPANET.

Thomas designed the computer worm as an experimentation tool that could replicate itself without causing harm. The intention was to demonstrate the functionality of mobile applications; instead, it damaged the DEC PDP-10 mainframe computers at Digital Equipment

Corporation, disrupting the linked teletype computer screens. On the screen, just the phrase "I'm the creeper, catch me if you can!" was displayed to the users.

The Reaper Program was developed in response to Thomas's colleague Ray Tomlinson. The Creeper was parallel to it. The Creeper discovers duplicates of itself as it travels the Internet and replicates. The duplicates are found, and then it logs them out, rendering them useless. The first cybersecurity effort, or antivirus software, was called The Reaper.

# Chapter 1

# What is Cybersecurity?

Cybersecurity prevents hostile assaults on computers, servers, mobile devices, electronic systems, networks, and data. It is often referred to as electronic information security or information technology security.

There are several basic areas into which the phrase "cybersecurity" can be subdivided and is used in a range of contexts, including business and mobile computing.

- ❖ **End-user instruction** considers the most erratic component of cyber-security: people. By disregarding sound security procedures, anyone might inadvertently introduce a virus into a system that is otherwise safe. For any firm to be secure, users must learn how to remove dubious email attachments, avoid plugging in unknown USB drives, and other crucial skills.

❖ **Business continuity and disaster recovery** specify how a company will react to a cyber-security breach or any other situation that results in the loss of data or operations. Disaster recovery plans specify how the company will reconstruct its data and activities to reach full operational capacity following an incident. Business continuity refers to the strategy that an organization uses to try to function in the absence of specific resources.

❖ **Security operations** incorporate the choices and procedures made for managing and safeguarding data assets. This includes the users' permissions when they access a network and the policies that dictate where and how data can be shared or stored.

❖ **Data protection** safeguards data privacy and integrity while it's being transferred and stored.

❖ **Security of applications** focuses on preventing attacks from entering devices and software. The data that an application is meant to secure could be accessed through compromise. Effective security starts long before a program or gadget is put into use, during the design phase.

❖ **Network safety** is the process of protecting a computer network from outsiders, such as opportunistic malware or targeted attackers.

## The extent of the cyber threat

There is an increasing number of data breaches every year, and the global cyber threat is still evolving at a rapid pace. According to a Risk

Based Security analysis, in just the first nine months of 2019, data breaches exposed an astounding 7.9 billion records. The amount of records revealed during the same period in 2018 is less than half (112%) of this statistic.

The majority of breaches occurred in the medical services, retail, and public sectors, and were caused by malevolent criminals. Because they gather financial and medical data, some of these industries are particularly attractive to cybercriminals; nonetheless, any company that uses a network might become the subject of consumer data breaches, corporate espionage, or customer attacks.

The amount spent globally on cybersecurity solutions is inevitably rising as the threat posed by cyberspace continues to grow in scope. By 2026, cybersecurity investment will have surpassed $260 billion worldwide, according to

Gartner, having reached $188.3 billion in 2023. Governments from all around the world have responded to the growing cyber threat by offering recommendations to businesses on how to adopt efficient cyber-security procedures. A cyber-security framework has been developed in the United States by the National Institute of Standards and Technology (NIST). The architecture suggests ongoing, real-time monitoring of all electronic resources to prevent the spread of dangerous code and facilitate early identification.

# Chapter 2

## Cyberthreat categories

Cybersecurity combats three types of threats:

1. The goal of cyberterrorism is to compromise electronic systems to incite fear or panic.

2. Cybercrime encompasses both individual and group targets who aim to disrupt or profit from systems.

3. Information gathering for political purposes is frequently a part of cyberattacks.

Thus, how do malevolent actors take over computer networks? The following are some typical techniques for endangering cybersecurity:

## A denial-of-service attack

Cybercriminals use denial-of-service attacks, in which they overload servers and networks with traffic to stop a computer system from responding to valid requests. This makes the system useless, which keeps a company from performing essential tasks.

## Attack by a man-in-the-middle

One kind of cyber danger is a man-in-the-middle attack, in which a cybercriminal eavesdrops on a conversation between two people to steal data. An attacker may, for instance, intercept data being transferred between the victim's device and the network using an insecure WiFi network.

## Phishing

Phishing is the practice of cybercriminals

requesting sensitive information from victims via emails that seem to be from a reputable company. Phishing attacks are frequently used to trick people into divulging personal information, including credit card numbers.

**Injection of SQL**

One kind of cyberattack used to take over and steal data from a database is called a SQL (structured language query) injection. Cybercriminals use weaknesses in data-driven applications to send malicious SQL statements into databases, inserting malicious code. They now have access to the database's sensitive data as a result.

**Malware**

Malicious software is referred to as malware. Malware, one of the most prevalent online dangers, is computer software designed by hackers or cybercriminals to harm or interfere with the operation of a normal user's computer. Malware is frequently distributed through unsolicited email attachments or downloads that appear authentic. Cybercriminals may use malware in financially motivated cyberattacks or to obtain political objectives.

Malware comes in many forms, such as the following:

- ❖ **Bot networks:** Cybercriminals employ networks of malware-infected machines to carry out online tasks without the consent of the user.

- ❖ **Ransomware:** Malware that threatens to erase a user's files and data unless a ransom is paid.

- ❖ **Adware:** Malware can be distributed through advertising software.

- ❖ **Spyware:** An application that surreptitiously logs user activity so that hackers might profit from it. Spyware, for instance, could record credit card information.

- ❖ **Virus:** A self-replicating malware that infects files with malicious code by attaching itself to clean files and propagating throughout a computer system.

- ❖ **Trojans:** A kind of malware that poses as trustworthy software. Cybercriminals deceive people into downloading Trojans, which then damage or gather data from their machines.

## Current threats from cyberspace

Which current cyber threats should people and organizations be on the lookout for? The governments of the United States, Australia, and the United Kingdom have released reports on some of the most recent cyber threats.

**Emotet malware**

The Australian Cyber Security Centre alerted national enterprises to a global cyber danger posed by the Emotet malware around the end of 2019.

A clever trojan, Emotet can load more software in addition to stealing data. Emotet is a reminder of the significance of creating a safe password to protect against cyber-attacks, as it thrives on simple passwords.

**Spyware called Dridex**

The head of a well-organized cybercrime ring was charged by the US Department of Justice (DoJ) in December 2019 for their involvement in the global Dridex malware assault. Worldwide, the people, government, infrastructure, and industry were all impacted by this malevolent campaign.

A financial trojan with a variety of features is called Dridex. It has been infecting users' PCs since 2014 and does so using phishing emails or pre-existing malware. It has resulted in enormous financial losses totaling hundreds of millions of dollars. It is capable of obtaining passwords, banking information, and personal data that can be used in fraudulent transactions.

Following the Dridex attacks, the National Cyber Security Centre in the United Kingdom is advising people to make sure their machines are patched, their anti-virus software is up to date, and their contents are backed up.

## End-user protection

One essential component of cyber security is end-user protection, sometimes known as endpoint security. After all, the end-user is frequently the one who inadvertently adds malware or another type of cyber threat on their mobile, laptop, or desktop computer.

In what ways do cyber-security measures safeguard systems and end users? The first step in cyber-security is the encryption of emails, files, and other important data using cryptographic algorithms. This prevents loss or theft in addition to safeguarding data while it's in transit.

Furthermore, PCs are scanned by end-user security software for harmful code, which is subsequently quarantined and deleted from the system. Safety apps are made to encrypt or erase data from a computer's hard disk and can even find and eliminate harmful code concealed in the primary boot record.

A key component of electronic security protocols is real-time malware detection. To protect against viruses or Trojan horses that transform into new forms with every execution—a.k.a. polymorphic and metamorphic malware—many employ heuristic and behavioral analysis to track the behavior of a program and its code. To study their behavior and improve their ability to identify new infections, security systems can isolate potentially dangerous programs from a user's network and confine them to a virtual bubble.

As cyber-security experts discover new threats and innovative ways to counter them, security programs never stop developing new defenses. Employees must be trained in the use of end-user security software to maximize its benefits. Most importantly, regular updates and maintenance guarantee that it can defend users from the most recent online attacks.

# Chapter 3

## How to Install a Secure Network at Home

A collection of gadgets that are connected to the internet and one another, such as gaming consoles, printers, smartphones, tablets, and wearable technology, is called a home network.

There are two ways to connect a home network:

✓ A wireless network that uses no cables to link gadgets like smartphones and tablets.

✓ Printers and scanners are connected over a wired network.

One crucial component of online safety is having a secure home network. Vulnerable networks can be used as a springboard by hackers to commit a variety of cybercrimes, including malware installation, identity and data theft, and botnet creation. To help you and your family use the internet safely, we walk you through the key actions you need to do to secure your home network in this tutorial.

## How to modify the default home network name

Changing the name of your network is the first step in securing your home network. The term for your network is called an SSID, or service set identifier. You can view a list of neighboring SSIDs by opening the Wi-Fi network list on your laptop or smartphone. For devices nearby to discover any open networks, routers broadcast SSIDs.

SSIDs have a maximum character count of 32. Manufacturers usually use a company name and a random combination of letters and numbers to produce default security identifications. Changing your SSID name is a smart idea since

- ✓ Since a non-generic name indicates that your router is more carefully managed than routers utilizing default generic names, it may deter hackers and network attackers.
- ✓ Criminals may be aware of the weaknesses in your router model and how to take advantage of them if they know who made it.

Modify the SSID to hide the router's model and

brand from view. Stay away from using an identity that contains any personal data, including your name, address, or phone number. It is advisable to choose a generic name for your network access point (SSID) so that hackers who are scrounging local Wi-Fi networks won't notice it.

**Make sure your router's password is strong.** Default passwords are usually pre-set on wireless routers. These are guessed by hackers, particularly if they are aware of your router's maker. Therefore, one way to improve home router security is to change your password as soon as you can. Usually, you may accomplish this by using your browser to access the router's administration interface. The address you enter should be the router's default IP address, which you can find on the bottom sticker or in the setup instructions.

A strong password consists of a combination of capital and lowercase letters, numbers, and symbols, and should be at least 12 characters long, if not longer. It is a good idea to update your password regularly, ideally every six months, for a safe home network.

**Fortify the Wi-Fi encryption.**

A crucial component of any Wi-Fi-protected setup is encryption. The encryption option included in the majority of wireless routers is typically disabled by default. Encryption on your home router can help keep your network safe. To encrypt transmissions so that only the user's device and the Wi-Fi router can read the contents, there are four common types of Wi-Fi protection systems.

They are as follows:
- ✓ Wired Equivalent Privacy (WEP)
- ✓ Wi-Fi Protected Access (WPA)
- ✓ Wi-Fi Protected Access 3 (WPA 3)
- ✓ Wi-Fi Protected Access 2 (WPA 2)

For individuals who are asking how to protect Wi-Fi, WPA 2 and WPA 3 are the better choices because they are more recent and safer. Brute force attacks can be used against the older versions of WEP and WPA.

If your router allows you to, think about setting up a guest wireless network that is password-protected and uses either WPA 2 or WPA 3. When guests arrive, use this guest network as your friends and family are unlikely to require or want to hack your network. Even so, it's possible that before utilizing your network, their devices were compromised or infected with malware. Adding a guest network to your home network improves its security.

**For further network security, use a VPN.** The primary purpose of virtual private networks, or VPNs, is to increase online privacy. VPNs encrypt your data to prevent hackers from knowing where you are or what you are doing online. Since the VPN uses the router to provide protection, even if the router's encryption is compromised, you can still encrypt your data with a VPN to render it unreadable.

A VPN can be useful if you're wondering how to secure your IP address. With the use of a VPN, you may pretend that you are using your device from somewhere other than your home address by changing your IP address. Devices such as

PCs, laptops, phones, and tablets can all use VPNs.

## Update the firmware on your router.

Keeping your software, including the firmware on your router, up to date is a smart cybersecurity practice. Hackers can take advantage of weaknesses in older firmware. A few routers may provide automated firmware upgrades, and others let users check for updates via the administrative interface. To find out whether updates are available for your router model, you can also visit the vendor's support page.

News reports about noteworthy virus attacks might occasionally serve as triggers for firmware updates. The maker of the router will be prompted to examine its firmware codes to make sure that its hardware is immune to the new assault in the event of a serious attack. Staying updated is necessary because if it is, they will release a security patch.

**To safeguard the devices on your network, use a firewall.**

Devices linked to your network are shielded from online hackers by a home firewall. By preventing internet-connected devices from accessing your network and enabling networked devices to connect to other internet-connected devices, they function as a one-way digital barrier. Make sure your network firewall is turned on; most routers have one turned on by default. To stop router attacks, you can install a reliable home firewall solution on your computer if your router lacks a firewall.

**Change the IP address of your router, if possible.**

Hackers find default router IP addresses easily. They are occasionally even available online. You can modify the address of your router to provide further defense against router attacks.

Go to the network settings or LAN/DHCP section of your router admin console by logging in. After altering your IP address, save. Take note of the updated address.

Merely changing a few digits ought to be adequate. After it has been modified, you can visit your router settings using the new address. You can reset your router to its original configuration if you ever need to change your IP address again.

**Create a different network just for IoT devices.**

The term "Internet of Things" (IoT) refers to

physical objects that are not computers, phones, or servers that are connected to the Internet and can gather and share data. Wearable fitness trackers, smart refrigerators, smart watches, and voice assistants like Google Home and Amazon Echo are a few examples of Internet of Things products.

There are cybersecurity implications with the Internet of Things:

- ✓ Not every Internet of Things gadget has a stellar security history.
- ✓ There are more possible points of entry for hackers the more devices there are online.

You might create a different Wi-Fi network specifically for your IoT devices if you want to increase router security and prevent router attacks. This is referred to as a virtual local area network or VLAN. By using a VLAN, you can make sure that your less secure Internet of Things devices are on a different network from your more valuable ones, such as laptops and phones, which hold the most sensitive data. This eliminates the possibility that your computers or phones could be compromised by hackers using unsecured IoT devices as possible entry points.

Since the majority of IoT devices are managed via smartphone apps that are linked to cloud services, using a VLAN does not restrict functionality. After their initial setup, the majority of these devices—if they have internet access—don't require direct local network communication with PCs or mobile phones.

**Disconnect the Universal Plug and Play.**

With the aid of Universal Plug and Play (UPnP), devices in your house may identify your network and then get in touch with their maker to receive supplies and software upgrades. Although UPnP is an essential component of the Internet of Things, hackers can infect devices using it and use them as part of botnets, which is bad. Malware programs can also leverage UPnP to get elevated access to the security configurations of your router.

For your household devices to be able to access the internet, your router needs to work with the UPnP system. These intelligent gadgets may present a security risk since many of them lack password protection or share the same password across all of their devices.

UPnP aids with device configuration, but once a device is operational, you should disable both its UPnP features and your router's UPnP compatibility

**To keep hackers out of your network, disable remote access.**

Numerous routers have functions intended to simplify remote access from outside your house. Nonetheless, you can typically securely disable these features from the router settings panel unless you want remote admin access to your router. You lower the possibility of someone remotely accessing and altering your network if you disable remote access.

Open the web interface on your router and search for the "Remote Access," "Remote Administration," or "Remote Management" capability to accomplish this. Make sure it is turned off; many routers have this turned off by default, but it is still advisable to double-check.

In the unlikely event that some of the devices and apps on your network turn out to require remote access, you can always reactivate the capability if necessary.

**Protect your network from unauthorized devices by using MAC address filtering.** Based on a device's MAC address, many routers let users limit which devices are permitted on their Wi-Fi networks. "Media access controller" is what MAC stands for, and a network device is identified by its MAC address. Attackers can't join a Wi-Fi network even if they know the password if MAC address filtering is enabled.

"MAC filtering," sometimes known as "MAC address filtering," is a menu item on the console of your router. A unique MAC address is assigned to each device that is capable of connecting to a network. Each device's address that you want to allow on your network must be located. Once you have that information, enter it into the router and activate the MAC address filtering feature.

**Consider the location of your router.**

Try to put your router in the middle of the room. This helps to conceal your network from hackers in addition to distributing network access more fairly. If at all possible, keep routers away from windows and exterior doors.

Recall that routers radiate not only horizontally but also vertically. To make sure that both the downstairs and the top floor of your two-story home are covered, set the router high on a shelf on the lower level.

**When you're not at home, turn off your network.**

Turning off your home network when you're not home is one of the simplest methods to keep it safe. When you're not at home, turning off your Wi-Fi lessens the likelihood that hackers may try to access your home network.

Unplugging the router when you're not using it lowers security concerns and shields it from power surge damage.

**Maintain the health of your devices.** Hackers may be able to access your router through the PCs and other devices in your house. Numerous gadgets linked to your network will be lightweight and portable, such as laptops, tablets, and smartphones. Because portable devices link to other networks and may use public Wi-Fi, they are more prone to become infected. Outside of your home, there is a higher chance of virus infection and hacking attempts. Since it is only exposed to one internet access point, equipment that is kept within your home is less likely to become infected. Recall to follow these best practices for cybersecurity to keep your home router secure:

✓ Ensure that your devices have a full suite of antivirus software installed. For instance, Kaspersky Premium guards your gadgets from malware, viruses, and hackers.

✓ Update your program and permit automatic updates. To fix security flaws, operating systems, and apps frequently receive patches and new versions.

✓ Secure devices with lengthy, complex passwords that are unique from one another. For this, a password manager can be useful.

# Chapter 4

# Effects of Cyberattacks on Businesses

1. **Losses of Money**

   Businesses may suffer greatly financially as a result of a cyberattack. Remedial expenses include paying for potential ransom payments, retrieving or replacing damaged systems, and employing cybersecurity specialists. Legal fees lost revenue from downtime, and fines for breaking data protection laws are examples of long-term expenditures.

2. **Disruptions to Operations**

Cyberattacks have the potential to seriously disrupt operations by bringing down systems or erasing important data. These interruptions may make it more difficult for a business to provide goods and services, lowering consumer satisfaction and possibly resulting in legal repercussions.

3. **Damage to Reputation**

A cyberattack has the potential to seriously harm a business's brand and cause investors, partners, and customers to lose faith in it. This may lead to a decline in sales and challenges in attracting new clients and obtaining funding.

## Cybersecurity's Growing Significance for Businesses

The significance of cybersecurity for organizations in the current digital era cannot be emphasized. Cyber threats are becoming more common and sophisticated due to our growing reliance on technology and the internet, which puts businesses of all sizes in danger. Here are some main arguments on why cybersecurity is so important to companies:

### Maintaining an Advantage Over Rivals

Businesses that put cybersecurity first are better positioned to maintain an advantage over rivals in the marketplace. Businesses can gain a competitive edge by focusing on their core skills and reducing the risk of cyber threats by putting strong security measures in place.

## Developing Customer Trust

Consumers are realizing more and more how important data security is. Establishing trust with customers through a strong commitment to cybersecurity can lead to improved loyalty and long-term connections for organizations.

## Adherence to Regulations

Companies must abide by a number of regulations that mandate them to uphold particular security standards in order to safeguard the information of their clients. Heavy fines and penalties may result from breaking these rules. Businesses may stay in compliance with these requirements and steer clear of possible legal problems by investing in cybersecurity.

## Sustaining Business Activities

Your company's activities may be disrupted by a cyberattack, leading to lost production and downtime. Making sure your business has a strong cybersecurity plan in place reduces the possibility of expensive disruptions and helps to preserve the continuity of your operations.

## Safeguarding            Private            Data

To safeguard sensitive data, one of the main reasons companies should invest in cybersecurity is this. Customer data, financial records, and confidential intellectual property are all included in this. Financial losses and harm to one's reputation are only two of the dire outcomes that may result from a cyberattack that compromises sensitive data.

# Chapter 5

# Why Cybersecurity Matters

The daily fabric of life is intricately interwoven with technology. The ways in which we live and work have altered as a result of digital platforms, from communication and entertainment to online banking and shopping. Although there are many advantages to these developments, there are also considerable risks. Consequently, cybersecurity has emerged as a crucial element in safeguarding people, organizations, and countries against potential risks that exist within the digital realm.

## Expanding Domains Result in Increased Vulnerability Touchpoints

Attackers have additional possible points of entry when more systems and devices are connected to the internet.

❖ **"Smart" Technology:** These days, commonplace appliances like refrigerators, security cameras, and thermostats may connect to the internet. Since many of these gadgets lack strong security measures, they are simple pickings. Some further fear that because electric cars rely heavily on computers, hackers will be able to easily hurt drivers by, for example, electronically turning the car off on an interstate and locking the steering wheel.

❖ **Work from Home:** The distinction between personal and professional networks has become hazier due to the trend of working from home. Vulnerabilities may arise because personal devices and home Wi-Fi networks may not have the same security procedures as business settings.

❖ **Cloud Processing:** Cloud services are essential to businesses for apps and storage. Unauthorized access to sensitive data stored in the cloud is possible if appropriate precautions are not in place. The efficiency of earlier security measures is progressively diminished by speedier AI, even in the case of multi-factor authentication.

**The Effects of Technological Development**
Digital technologies are being adopted quickly, and this has transformed several industries. Healthcare providers employ electronic records to give improved patient care, businesses use data analytics to make decisions, and educational institutions provide online learning opportunities. However, the increased adoption

of digital technologies also creates new opportunities for cyberattacks.

## Emerging Technologies' Significance

New instruments in the battle against cyber dangers are brought about by emerging technologies. By bringing cutting-edge techniques for threat detection and response, artificial intelligence and machine learning are revolutionizing cybersecurity.

Artificial intelligence examines vast volumes of data to spot odd trends that could point to a cyberattack. By using advanced threat detection, organizations may identify possible problems before they become more serious. Systems that use machine learning can respond to new threats and adapt to them far more quickly than human operators. Real-time mitigation of assaults by automated reactions can lessen the impact on data and systems.

Additionally, blockchain technology greatly enhances cybersecurity. Stronger data security is provided by its decentralized structure, which makes it harder for unauthorized parties to alter data. By providing a safe platform for transactions, this technology lowers the possibility of fraud. Blockchain provides an additional degree of security to digital transactions by making sure that every transaction is recorded and validated at many locations.

# Chapter 6

# The Protective Role of Cybersecurity Experts

Cybersecurity experts are essential in preventing threats to personal and business data. They employ a variety of techniques and resources to guarantee the security of information.

## Planning for Incident Response

Effective handling of cyber incidents requires preparation. Professionals in cybersecurity create well-defined plans for handling security breaches, including recovery and communication tactics. They ensure that backups are set up to minimize downtime and data loss by enabling speedy restoration of systems and data. Organizations can smoothly recover from any disturbances with the aid of this proactive approach.

## Hazard Assessment

These experts examine systems on a regular basis to find and address vulnerabilities. They remain ahead of such risks by regularly assessing software and networks. Reducing risks can be achieved by putting security measures like firewalls, access controls, and encryption into place. By strengthening the barriers surrounding sensitive data, these safeguards increase the difficulty of unauthorized parties gaining access.

## Community Advancement

- ❖ **Youth Initiatives:** Introducing cybersecurity ideas to students can motivate the following generation of professionals.

- ❖ **Programs for Education:** Cybersecurity professionals make training investments to provide people with the abilities they need to defend against attacks.

❖ **Participation in the Community:** Public education regarding fundamental cybersecurity procedures can stop a lot of frequent attacks.

❖ **Constant Education:** Experts are urged to keep abreast of the most recent advancements in cybersecurity.

# Chapter 7

## Future Prospects for Cybersecurity

How firms will be safeguarded from hackers through technology

Since 1971, when the first computer virus was created, cybersecurity has existed. The virus in question was known as the "creeper," an innocuous program that spreads from computer to computer by replication. But every day, "threat actors" try to create new tools for often nefarious goals, which results in new malware being generated.

Cybersecurity experts try to thwart them, competing with one another in an increasingly competitive endeavor.

The complexity of the game has grown throughout the years on both sides.

Both sides are using AI and machine learning to keep playing this game of cat and mouse. Next up will be quantum computing, which will significantly increase both attacker and defensive capabilities. Thus, the game will not drastically change overall, but the cat and mouse will continue to improve and move more quickly.

This is how cybersecurity will develop in the future.

**A rise in automation**

Technology to enable effective cybersecurity operations. It's only a matter of scale. The key to successful cyber warfare will always be humans - competent human minds acting as the mouse or the cat. However, there are simply too many threats to keep an eye on, too many vectors, too many targets, and too many threat varieties (there are presently easily over a billion infections). It has to be made simpler. Before all of that data is delivered to human security experts, machine learning and artificial intelligence are already being used to help make sense of it.

Attackers are cognizant of the limitations inherent in computers. Hackers frequently use this technique to divert attention by putting false or misleading events on security experts' screens. With the best tools, even the most skilled analysts will eventually get overwhelmed. This has been greatly aided by the cloud, which has reduced costs and increased scalability, making it possible to use. Another important factor will be quantum computing, which will aid in sorting through complicated situations and predicting or identifying even minute signs of a hazard.

## Safe remote entry

The necessity to provide remote access security has arisen from the recent transition to remote working. In light of a highly distributed infrastructure, businesses need to reconsider their security strategies. Attackers are adapting their strategy in the meantime, figuring out how to go after workers who are isolated from the company but are yet linked to the network. The cybersecurity sector has been equipped to keep important jobs physically and fully apart by decades-old best practices in operational technology. A crucial distant worker, for instance, might have a single-purpose laptop with limited functionality that cannot be used for anything other than that task. It also won't have any access to social media, email, or public network connections.

## Additional concerns about ransomware

For several years, ransomware has been gradually becoming one of the most common cyber threats, if not the most common. Over the years, ransomware has grown increasingly powerful and common. It has consequently also grown to be very effective. The organizations behind ransomware campaigns directly profit financially from their efforts. In addition to encrypting a target's data, ransomware is increasingly being used in broader attack campaigns. Preemptively targeting backup and recovery tools, adversaries try to thwart data recovery procedures. That pattern will not change.

**USBs will pose a greater risk.**

There are USB gadgets everywhere. Individuals are accustomed to seeing, utilizing, and possessing them. To compromise industrial targets, threat actors frequently target USBs. According to our most current USB threat report,

19% of the threats uncovered were intended to use USB-detachable devices in some capacity. Threats from USB to industrials increased to 59%, more than doubling. Many people have a propensity to undervalue "malware." For the majority of non-techies, the annoying spyware or adware on your computer is referred to as a "virus."

However, malware can be far more hazardous and serious. In some OT situations, this might result in a loss of perspective, which makes operators blind to the process and unable to adequately monitor circumstances. That is extremely risky in industrial settings with high levels of danger. Malware can also result in process loss by directly harming or terminating a process. According to our most recent USB threat report, the quantity of high-impact malware has increased.

In the end, in-depth cybersecurity protection plans won't disappear. An organization can't eliminate the danger of a cyberattack; instead, it must implement a variety of technologies and procedures to help ensure that the hazards are as low as possible.